"10 Proven Strategies for Making Money on YouTube"

Introduction

Welcome to "10 Proven Strategies for Making Money on YouTube," your comprehensive guide to turning your passion for creating videos into a profitable online venture. In the dynamic world of digital content creation, YouTube stands as an unparalleled platform that not only fosters creativity but also offers substantial income potential. This ebook is your roadmap to navigating the YouTube landscape successfully.

In the following pages, we will delve into a wealth of strategies, insights, and expert advice garnered from successful YouTubers who have turned their channels into lucrative businesses. Whether you're a seasoned content creator or just starting your journey, this ebook is designed to equip you with the tools and knowledge needed to monetize your content effectively.

From optimising your channel and engaging with your audience to exploring various revenue streams and staying up-to-date with the latest trends, we'll cover it all. Each strategy presented here is tried, tested, and proven to work, ensuring that you can build a sustainable income from your YouTube endeavours.

So, if you're ready to transform your passion into profit and unlock the full potential of your YouTube channel, let's dive into these ten proven strategies that will help you achieve financial success while doing what you love. Your journey to YouTube prosperity starts now.

Index

1. Content Niche Selection: Begin by choosing a specific content niche that aligns with your interests and expertise. Focusing on a niche helps you attract a dedicated audience.
2. Quality Content Creation: Invest in high-quality video production, including camera equipment, editing software, and scripting to create engaging and informative content.

3. SEO Optimization: Master YouTube's search engine optimization (SEO) by using relevant keywords, captivating titles, and detailed descriptions to enhance discoverability.
4. Audience Engagement: Foster a strong connection with your viewers by actively responding to comments, asking for feedback, and creating a sense of community on your channel.
5. Monetization Features: Explore YouTube's monetization options, such as AdSense, channel memberships, and merchandise shelf integration to generate income.
6. Affiliate Marketing: Partner with brands and promote their products or services in your videos, earning a commission for every sale generated through your unique affiliate links.
7. Sponsorships and Brand Deals: Collaborate with companies relevant to your niche for sponsored content opportunities, providing an additional income stream.
8. Crowdfunding and Donations: Utilise platforms like Patreon or set up donation links to allow your loyal audience to support your channel financially.
9. Diversify Platforms: Expand your online presence by repurposing your content on other social media platforms and driving traffic back to your YouTube channel.
10. Consistency and Adaptation: Maintain a consistent upload schedule while staying updated with YouTube trends and algorithm changes to ensure long-term growth and revenue

Chapter-1

Content Niche Selection: Begin by choosing a specific content niche that aligns with your interests and expertise. Focusing on a niche helps you attract a dedicated audience.

Content Niche Selection: The Key to YouTube Success
In the ever-expanding realm of YouTube, where content is king, selecting the right niche is akin to choosing the foundation for your digital empire. Whether you aspire to be the next gaming sensation, a culinary maestro, a fashion guru, or an educational authority, beginning

with a well-defined content niche is the bedrock upon which your YouTube journey is built.

Understanding the Importance of a Content Niche

A content niche is essentially the subject or theme around which your YouTube channel revolves. It is the heart and soul of your content strategy, and its significance cannot be overstated. Why, you might ask? Let's delve into the intricacies.

Alignment with Interests and Expertise

To embark on this journey, begin by seeking the nexus of your interests and expertise. Your content niche should resonate with your passions and knowledge. After all, the adage "do what you love" holds true in the world of YouTube, perhaps even more so than anywhere else. When you create content in a niche that genuinely captivates your interest, your enthusiasm will be palpable. Your viewers will sense it, and this authentic passion will magnetise them. They're more likely to subscribe, engage, and return for more. Your own zest for the subject will be contagious.

Appealing to a Dedicated Audience

Focusing on a niche doesn't just align your content with your personal interests; it also helps you attract a dedicated audience. When you tailor your videos to a specific topic or theme, you naturally draw in viewers who share that interest. This is the essence of building a niche community. Whether it's vintage car restoration, organic gardening, or makeup tutorials, your niche becomes a magnet for those who are genuinely enthusiastic about the subject matter. They're not casual viewers; they're passionate fans. And passionate fans are more likely to support your channel in various ways – from subscribing to buying your merchandise or supporting you on platforms like Patreon.

Setting Yourself Apart

In the vast ocean of YouTube content, standing out can be a daunting challenge. However, focusing on a niche is like hoisting a flag that signals your uniqueness. By becoming the go-to channel for a specific topic, you establish yourself as an authority or enthusiast in that field. This distinguishes you from the multitudes of creators who produce a mishmash of content.

Think of it this way: if you were a budding chef, would you be more inclined to follow a general cooking channel that occasionally dabbles in baking, grilling, and cocktail mixing, or would you prefer a channel wholly devoted to the art of perfecting sourdough bread? The specialised channel not only demonstrates a deeper knowledge but also provides a more targeted and valuable experience for the viewer. It's this distinctiveness that fosters loyalty.

Monetizing Your Niche

Once you've established your niche and cultivated a dedicated following, the path to monetization becomes more accessible. Your engaged audience is more likely to respond positively to revenue-generating strategies. Whether it's through ad revenue, affiliate marketing, sponsorships, or merchandise sales, a niche-focused channel provides a more fertile ground for income generation.

The Bottom Line

In conclusion, the importance of content niche selection cannot be overstated in your YouTube journey. It's the compass that guides your content creation, the magnet that attracts a passionate audience, and the flag that signals your uniqueness in a crowded digital landscape.

So, whether you're passionate about tech reviews, wildlife photography, fitness tips, or any other subject under the sun, remember that selecting the right content niche is your first step towards YouTube success. Align your interests and expertise, create captivating content, and watch your channel thrive as you connect with a dedicated community of like-minded enthusiasts. In the world of YouTube, your niche is your key to unlocking a world of opportunities, all while doing what you love. British English has never sounded more promising on YouTube.

Chapter-2

Quality Content Creation: Invest in high-quality video production, including camera equipment, editing software, and scripting to create engaging and informative content.

Quality Content Creation: Elevating Your YouTube Channel

In the captivating realm of YouTube, the phrase "quality over quantity" is more than just a catchy slogan; it's the cornerstone of success. To truly stand out and engage your audience, it's imperative to invest in high-quality video production. This investment encompasses several critical components, from camera equipment and editing software to the art of scripting, all with the ultimate aim of creating content that is both engaging and informative.

Camera Equipment: The Lens Through Which Your Story Is Told

Your choice of camera equipment is pivotal in shaping the visual narrative of your YouTube channel. While smartphones have come a long way in terms of video quality, investing in a dedicated camera can take your content to the next level. High-end DSLRs or mirrorless cameras are popular choices among content creators for their versatility and exceptional image quality.

However, it's not just about the camera body; the selection of lenses plays a crucial role in capturing the perfect shot. Different lenses offer varied perspectives and artistic possibilities, enabling you to convey your message effectively. Whether it's a wide-angle lens for immersive landscapes or a prime lens for crisp portraits, your camera equipment becomes the palette with which you paint your YouTube canvas.

Editing Software: Sculpting Your Vision

Once you've captured your footage, the editing process is where the magic truly happens. Editing software empowers you to refine your content, adding layers of creativity and professionalism. There are various editing programs available, catering to a range of skill levels and budgets. From Adobe Premiere Pro to Final Cut Pro, the choice is yours.

Editing allows you to weave your narrative seamlessly, incorporating transitions, overlays, and effects that captivate your viewers. A well-edited video not only keeps your audience engaged but also communicates your message with clarity and impact. It's the final polish that transforms raw footage into a compelling story.

Scripting: The Backbone of Your Content

Behind every great YouTube video lies a well-crafted script. Scripting is the process of planning and organising your content, outlining key points, and ensuring a coherent flow. Whether you're creating educational tutorials, entertaining vlogs, or persuasive product reviews, a script keeps you on track and ensures that your message is clear and concise.

Scripts also enhance your delivery, helping you avoid stumbling or going off-topic. While spontaneity has its place, scripted content often appears more professional and polished. It allows you to convey your expertise confidently and engage your audience effectively.

The Art of Engagement: Creating Content that Resonates

High-quality content isn't just about technical prowess; it's also about creating videos that resonate with your audience. Understanding your viewers' preferences, pain points, and interests is essential. Conducting research and staying attuned to current trends can help you tailor your content to meet their expectations.

Moreover, engagement extends beyond video production. Interacting with your audience through comments, social media, and live streams fosters a sense of community and loyalty. It's the human touch that can turn casual viewers into devoted subscribers.

Monetizing Your Investment

While investing in high-quality video production does incur costs, it also opens doors to various monetization opportunities. Ads served on your videos generate revenue, and a professional image can attract brand sponsorships. Your investment in quality equipment and software positions you as a serious content creator, making you more appealing to potential collaborators and advertisers.

Conclusion: Quality as a Path to Success

In the competitive world of YouTube, quality content creation is your secret weapon. It elevates your channel above the rest, captivating your audience and setting the stage for monetization opportunities. With the right camera equipment, editing software, and scripting, you can transform your passion into captivating, informative, and visually stunning videos that resonate with viewers in the realm of British English on YouTube. Remember, it's not just about what you say, but how you say it, and the quality of your production can speak volumes.

Chapter-3

SEO Optimization: Master YouTube's search engine optimization (SEO) by using relevant keywords, captivating titles, and detailed descriptions to enhance discoverability.

SEO Optimization on YouTube: Your Path to Discoverability

In the bustling universe of YouTube, where millions of videos compete for attention, mastering Search Engine Optimization (SEO) is akin to unlocking a treasure chest of discoverability. SEO on YouTube involves a meticulous strategy that employs relevant keywords, captivating titles, and detailed descriptions to ensure your content stands out and reaches the right audience. In the context of British English, let's delve into the importance and nuances of YouTube SEO.

The Significance of YouTube SEO

Consider this scenario: you've put your heart and soul into creating a stellar video – it's informative, entertaining, and beautifully produced. Yet, without effective SEO, your masterpiece may remain hidden in the depths of YouTube's vast archive. SEO is the beacon that guides viewers to your content, making it an indispensable tool for creators.

Keywords: The Building Blocks of SEO

At the core of YouTube SEO are keywords – those words and phrases that encapsulate the essence of your video. Start by conducting meticulous keyword research to identify the terms and phrases that are relevant to your content. Tools like YouTube's own search suggest feature, Google's Keyword Planner, and third-party applications can assist in this quest.

Once you've amassed a collection of pertinent keywords, strategically incorporate them into your video's metadata. This includes your video title, description, and tags. Be mindful of maintaining a natural and coherent flow; keyword stuffing, where keywords are excessively repeated, is discouraged and can harm your search ranking.

Captivating Titles: The First Impression

Your video's title is often the first point of contact between your content and potential viewers. It's your chance to entice, intrigue, and inform. A well-crafted title should incorporate your target keywords while still being attention-grabbing and relevant.

For instance, if you've created a tutorial on vegan baking, a title like "Delicious Vegan Baking Recipes | How to Bake Without Eggs" combines keywords ("vegan baking,""recipes") with an engaging promise ("delicious") and a solution to a common query ("how to bake without eggs"). Crafting titles that strike this balance is an art in itself.

Detailed Descriptions: Providing Context

The video description is your canvas for providing context and additional information. In British English, craft a comprehensive and engaging description that not only outlines the content but also elaborates on the keywords you're targeting. Include relevant links, timestamps, and any resources mentioned in the video.

Consider writing a brief paragraph at the beginning of your description that provides a captivating preview of your video's content. This entices viewers to continue reading and, ideally, watch your video. A well-structured description is not only valuable for SEO but also for viewer engagement.

Tags: Enhancing Discoverability

Tags are like signposts that guide YouTube's algorithm to understand the content of your video. Use a mix of broad and specific tags related to your niche and target keywords. While tags are not as prominently displayed as titles and descriptions, they play a crucial role in improving your video's discoverability.

Engagement and Audience Retention: The SEO Ecosystem

YouTube's algorithm is a complex ecosystem, and SEO is just one component. It rewards videos that keep viewers engaged and on the platform. Factors like watch time, audience retention, likes, comments, and shares all influence your video's ranking. Therefore, it's vital to create content that not only attracts viewers but also keeps them hooked.

Consistency and Adaptation: The SEO Journey

Finally, remember that SEO on YouTube is an ongoing journey. Trends, algorithms, and viewer preferences evolve. Consistency in producing high-quality content and a willingness to adapt to these changes are key to long-term success in the world of YouTube.

In the British English context, mastering YouTube's SEO is not just about algorithms; it's about ensuring your content finds its rightful place among a discerning audience. It's the art of being discoverable in a vast sea of digital content, where the right keywords, titles, descriptions, and engagement strategies act as the compass guiding viewers to your channel.

Chapter-4

Audience Engagement: Foster a strong connection with your viewers by actively responding to comments, asking for feedback, and creating a sense of community on your channel.

Audience Engagement on YouTube: Building a Thriving Community

In the vibrant realm of YouTube, where creators vie for viewers' attention, audience engagement stands as a potent catalyst for success. The essence of audience engagement lies in fostering a strong connection with your viewers, transforming them from passive observers into an active and devoted community. In the context of British English, let's explore the significance of audience engagement and the strategies to create a thriving YouTube community.

The Heartbeat of Your Channel
Your viewers are not just numbers on a screen; they are the lifeblood of your channel. Engaging with your audience is more than a mere courtesy; it's a strategic imperative. It cultivates loyalty, encourages interaction, and paves the way for sustained growth.

Active Comment Response
One of the most immediate ways to engage with your audience is by actively responding to comments on your videos. This demonstrates that you value and appreciate your viewers' input. Whether it's a question, a compliment, or constructive criticism, acknowledging and responding to comments strengthens the bond between creator and viewer.

In the context of British English, maintaining a polite and friendly tone in your responses is crucial. A simple "Thank you for your comment!" or a thoughtful reply to a viewer's query can go a long way in building a positive relationship.

Feedback-Seeking Behaviour
Invite your audience to be a part of your creative journey by actively seeking their feedback. Pose questions, conduct polls, or request suggestions for future content. This not only empowers your audience to influence your content but also makes them feel invested in your channel's growth.

For instance, if your channel revolves around travel vlogs, you might ask your viewers for destination recommendations or travel tips. This kind of engagement fosters a sense of community and inclusivity, as your viewers become co-creators of your content.

Creating a Sense of Community
Building a community on YouTube is more than just producing videos; it's about creating a virtual space where viewers feel a sense of belonging. Here are some strategies to achieve this:

1. **Establish a Consistent Presence:** Regular uploads and live streams, if feasible, create a sense of anticipation among your audience.

They know when to expect new content and can plan their engagement accordingly.

2. **Develop a Unique Channel Identity:** Your channel should have a distinct personality and theme. This makes it easier for viewers to connect with your content on a personal level.

3. **Collaborate with Your Community:** Involve your audience in your content creation process. Host Q&A sessions, feature user-submitted content, or even bring viewers on as guests in your videos.

4. **Moderate Your Community:** Maintain a respectful and positive environment by moderating comments and addressing any toxicity promptly. A friendly and welcoming atmosphere encourages more meaningful engagement.

5. **Utilise Social Media:** Extend your community-building efforts beyond YouTube by actively engaging with your audience on social media platforms like Instagram, Twitter, or a dedicated Facebook group.

The Impact of Engagement on Growth

Audience engagement is not just a feel-good exercise; it's a strategic driver of growth. When viewers feel valued and connected to your channel, they are more likely to subscribe, like, share, and return for more. Moreover, engaged viewers tend to be more loyal, making them advocates for your content within their own networks.

Engagement also has a positive impact on YouTube's algorithm, which rewards videos with higher levels of interaction and watch time. This means that engaged viewers can contribute to your videos being recommended to a broader audience.

Conclusion: Nurturing Your YouTube Community

In conclusion, audience engagement is the cornerstone of a successful YouTube channel. Building a thriving community is not only rewarding but also strategic for long-term growth. In British English, it's about creating a welcoming and inclusive space where viewers feel heard, valued, and connected. So, embrace your audience, respond to their comments, seek their input, and cultivate a vibrant YouTube community that propels your channel to new heights.

Chapter-5

Monetization Features: Explore YouTube's monetization options, such as AdSense, channel

memberships, and merchandise shelf integration to generate income.

Monetization Features on YouTube: Turning Passion into Profit
In the dynamic landscape of YouTube, where creators continuously craft compelling content, monetization features serve as the bridge between creative passion and financial reward. For creators on YouTube, the opportunities to generate income are vast, and understanding and leveraging these monetization features can transform a hobby into a sustainable career. In the context of British English, let's delve into the essential aspects of YouTube monetization.

Unlocking Revenue Streams
YouTube offers creators several avenues for monetizing their content, allowing them to reap the financial rewards of their hard work and dedication. Here are some key monetization features:

1. AdSense: Leveraging the Power of Advertising
The most accessible and widely-used monetization feature on YouTube is AdSense. AdSense allows creators to earn revenue from ads displayed before, during, or after their videos. These ads can take the form of skippable video ads, non-skippable video ads, display ads, or overlay ads.

To enable AdSense on your channel, you need to meet specific eligibility criteria, including having at least 1,000 subscribers and 4,000 hours of watch time in the past 12 months. Once enabled, YouTube will share a portion of the ad revenue generated by your content.

In the British English context, it's important to note that viewers from various regions may see different ads based on their location and preferences, which can impact your ad revenue.

2. Channel Memberships: Building a Dedicated Fan Base
Channel memberships offer a direct and interactive way to monetize your YouTube channel. For a monthly fee, subscribers become members of your channel, gaining access to perks like custom badges, emojis, and members-only content. This feature fosters a sense of community and loyalty among your most dedicated viewers.

To enable channel memberships, you must meet specific eligibility requirements, including having at least 30,000 subscribers. Once activated, you can tailor the membership experience to suit your audience, creating a unique and rewarding environment for your members.

3. Merchandise Shelf Integration: Turning Fans into Customers

The merchandise shelf integration is a valuable tool for creators with a line of branded merchandise. It allows you to showcase your products directly beneath your YouTube videos, making it easy for viewers to explore and purchase items related to your channel.

Integrating your merchandise shelf requires setting up a compatible merch store and complying with YouTube's merchandise policies. This feature not only generates income but also reinforces your brand identity and fosters a deeper connection with your audience.

Other Monetization Options

Beyond these primary monetization features, there are other income-generating strategies to explore:

- ****Super Chat and Super Stickers:**** During live streams, viewers can purchase Super Chat messages and Super Stickers to have their messages stand out. Creators receive a share of the revenue generated by these interactions.

- ****YouTube Premium Revenue:**** When YouTube Premium subscribers watch your content, you earn a portion of the revenue based on their watch time.

- ****Sponsored Content:**** Collaborating with brands for sponsored content can provide a substantial source of income. Ensure that sponsorships align with your channel's niche and audience to maintain authenticity.

- ****Affiliate Marketing:**** Promoting products or services through affiliate links in your video descriptions can generate income through commissions on sales generated.

Strategies for Maximising Monetization

To make the most of these monetization features, consider the following strategies:

1. Diversify Income Streams: Don't rely on a single monetization method. Diversify your income sources to reduce dependence on a single revenue stream.

2. Engage with Your Audience: Build a loyal and engaged audience by responding to comments, fostering a sense of community, and seeking feedback.

3. Quality Over Quantity: Prioritise the quality of your content. High-quality videos tend to attract more viewers and generate better ad revenue.

4. Stay Compliant: Familiarise yourself with YouTube's policies and guidelines to avoid potential issues that could impact your monetization.
5. Market Your Merchandise: If you use the merchandise shelf, actively promote your products in your videos and live streams to boost sales.
Conclusion: Monetization for British Creators
In the world of YouTube, monetization features are the key to transforming creative passion into a sustainable income. Understanding and strategically using these features can turn your channel into a thriving source of revenue, allowing you to continue doing what you love while building a successful career in British English. Explore the possibilities, engage with your audience, and maximise your monetization potential on YouTube.

Chapter-6

Affiliate Marketing: Partner with brands and promote their products or services in your videos, earning a commission for every sale generated through your unique affiliate links.

Affiliate Marketing on YouTube: Turning Recommendations into Revenue
In the ever-evolving landscape of YouTube, content creators are discovering innovative ways to transform their passion into profit. Affiliate marketing has emerged as a lucrative strategy, enabling creators to partner with brands and promote their products or services within their videos. In return, creators earn a commission for every sale generated through their unique affiliate links. In the context of British English, let's delve into the nuances of affiliate marketing and how it can empower creators to monetize their YouTube channels.
Affiliate Marketing Unveiled
At its core, affiliate marketing is a symbiotic partnership between content creators and brands. Creators leverage their influence and reach to endorse products or services, while brands gain exposure to a targeted and engaged audience. The linchpin of this collaboration is the affiliate link, a trackable URL unique to each creator. When viewers

click on this link and make a purchase, the creator earns a percentage of the sale as a commission.

Selecting the Right Affiliate Partners

The success of affiliate marketing hinges on choosing the right partners. Creators should align themselves with brands that resonate with their channel's niche and are relevant to their audience. For instance, a tech reviewer might collaborate with companies specialising in gadgets, while a fashion vlogger could partner with clothing brands. The key is to maintain authenticity and ensure that promoted products or services genuinely benefit your viewers.

In British English, it's essential to clearly disclose your affiliate relationships to maintain transparency and build trust with your audience. You can do this through verbal disclaimers in your videos or by including a written disclosure in the video description.

Crafting Engaging Affiliate Content

The art of affiliate marketing lies in seamlessly integrating product or service recommendations into your content. Here's how to do it effectively:

1. Value First: Prioritise delivering value to your viewers. Your primary goal is to provide helpful and informative content that addresses their needs or interests. The affiliate promotion should be a natural extension of this value.

2. Genuine Endorsement: Only endorse products or services that you genuinely believe in and have personally tested. Your authenticity and credibility are paramount.

3. Educate and Demonstrate: Show your audience how the product or service solves a problem or enhances their lives. Demonstrate its features and benefits in a relatable manner.

4. Call to Action: Encourage viewers to take action by clicking on your affiliate link. Clearly explain the benefits they'll receive by doing so, such as discounts or exclusive offers.

Maximising Affiliate Revenue

To maximise your affiliate marketing revenue, consider the following strategies:

1. Strategic Placement: Position your affiliate promotions at relevant points in your videos. For instance, if you're reviewing a camera, place the affiliate link when discussing its features or showing sample footage.

14

2. Utilise Multiple Platforms: Promote your affiliate links across various platforms, such as your YouTube channel, website, and social media accounts. This expands your reach and potential for earnings.
3. Track and Optimise: Use tracking tools provided by affiliate programs to monitor the performance of your links. Analyse which products or services resonate most with your audience and optimise your strategy accordingly.
4. Create Compelling Content: Craft engaging and persuasive content that compels viewers to take action. This may involve storytelling, problem-solving, or highlighting the product's unique selling points.

The Ethical Dimension
In British English and across the YouTube community, maintaining ethical standards is essential in affiliate marketing. Transparency, honesty, and integrity should underpin your approach. If you receive compensation for promoting a product or service, it's imperative to disclose this information clearly to your audience. Such transparency builds trust and ensures that your recommendations are genuine.

Conclusion: Affiliate Marketing as a Revenue Stream
In conclusion, affiliate marketing offers creators on YouTube a potent avenue for monetizing their channels while delivering value to their viewers. By forging authentic partnerships with relevant brands, crafting engaging affiliate content, and maintaining transparency, creators can harness the power of affiliate marketing in the realm of British English on YouTube. Ultimately, it's a win-win, where creators earn commissions, brands gain exposure, and viewers discover valuable products or services.

Chapter-7

Sponsorships and Brand Deals: Collaborate with companies relevant to your niche for sponsored content opportunities, providing an additional income stream.

Sponsorships and Brand Deals on YouTube: Cultivating Profitable Collaborations
In the dynamic world of YouTube content creation, one avenue that has become increasingly significant for creators seeking to monetize their channels is sponsorships and brand deals. This strategy involves

collaborating with companies or brands relevant to your niche to produce sponsored content, providing an additional income stream. In British English, let's explore the intricacies of sponsorships and brand deals, and how they can empower creators to turn their passion into profit.

The Essence of Sponsorships and Brand Deals

Sponsorships and brand deals are a form of influencer marketing, where creators partner with companies or brands to endorse their products or services within their content. This endorsement typically takes the shape of dedicated videos, mentions, or integrations seamlessly woven into the creator's existing content.

In these collaborations, creators act as a bridge between the brand and their dedicated audience. Brands benefit from the creator's reach, trust, and connection with their viewers, while creators gain financial compensation for promoting the products or services. The success of such partnerships relies on the authenticity and relevance of the endorsement to the creator's niche and audience.

Selecting the Right Collaborations

Choosing the right sponsorships and brand deals is paramount to maintaining credibility and resonance with your audience. Consider the following factors when evaluating potential collaborations:

1. Relevance: The brand or product should align with your channel's niche and the interests of your viewers. A seamless fit enhances the authenticity of the endorsement.

2. Authenticity: Only collaborate with brands or products you genuinely believe in and can endorse honestly. Authenticity builds trust with your audience.

3. Quality: Assess the quality of the brand's products or services. Promoting subpar offerings can damage your reputation.

4. Audience Match: Analyse whether the brand's target audience aligns with your own. Brands are often interested in reaching audiences similar to yours.

The Art of Sponsored Content

Creating sponsored content that resonates with your audience requires a delicate touch. Here's how to craft effective sponsored content:

1. Integration: Seamlessly integrate the brand or product into your content rather than making it the focal point. This ensures that the endorsement feels natural and relevant to your audience.

2. Education: Educate your viewers about the brand or product by highlighting its benefits, features, and how it addresses their needs or interests. Consider demonstrating its use in a practical context.

3. Storytelling: Weave a compelling narrative around the brand or product. Tell a story that illustrates its value or impact in a relatable manner.

4. Honesty: Maintain transparency by clearly disclosing that the content is sponsored. Honesty is key to preserving trust with your audience.

Negotiating Sponsorships and Compensation

The terms of sponsorships and brand deals can vary widely. Negotiating fair compensation is a critical aspect of successful collaborations. Factors that influence compensation include:

1. Reach and Engagement: The size and engagement of your audience play a significant role in determining your value to brands. Creators with larger, more engaged followings often command higher fees.

2. Content Scope: The scope of the sponsored content, such as video duration, complexity, and exclusivity, can impact compensation.

3. Brand Reputation: Collaborating with reputable brands may lead to higher compensation due to the perceived value of association.

4. Deliverables: Clarify the specific deliverables expected from the collaboration, including the number of videos, social media posts, or other promotional activities.

Ethical Considerations

Maintaining ethical standards is paramount in sponsorships and brand deals. Creators should be transparent with their audience about the nature of the collaboration and any financial compensation received. Such transparency fosters trust and ensures that viewers can make informed decisions about the content they consume.

Conclusion: Sponsorships as a Revenue Stream

In conclusion, sponsorships and brand deals offer YouTube creators a valuable avenue for generating income while delivering relevant content to their audience. By selecting the right collaborations, crafting authentic and engaging content, and negotiating fair compensation, creators can leverage sponsorships to monetize their channels effectively in the realm of British English on YouTube. Ultimately, it's a mutually beneficial relationship where brands gain exposure and credibility, creators earn revenue, and viewers discover products or services tailored to their interests.

Chapter-8

Crowdfunding and Donations: Utilise platforms like Patreon or set up donation links to allow your loyal audience to support your channel financially.

Crowdfunding and Donations on YouTube: Empowering Creators through Viewer Support

In the ever-evolving landscape of YouTube content creation, crowdfunding and donations have emerged as powerful tools for creators seeking to transform their passion into a sustainable career. By leveraging platforms like Patreon or setting up donation links, creators can invite their loyal audience to support their channel financially. In the context of British English, let's delve into the intricacies of crowdfunding and donations, and how they empower creators to continue producing valuable content.

The Essence of Crowdfunding and Donations

Crowdfunding and donations represent a direct financial relationship between creators and their viewers. These platforms enable creators to seek financial contributions, often on a recurring basis, from their audience in exchange for various perks or simply as a gesture of support.

While crowdfunding platforms like Patreon offer a structured way to provide exclusive content or rewards to supporters, setting up donation links provides a straightforward method for viewers to make one-time or recurring contributions. Both options allow creators to diversify their income streams beyond traditional ad revenue.

Connecting with Your Audience

One of the most significant advantages of crowdfunding and donations is the sense of community and connection they foster between creators and their audience. Viewers who choose to support creators through these channels often feel a deeper sense of involvement and investment in the content they love.

Creators can use these platforms to offer various perks or rewards to their supporters, such as early access to videos, exclusive behind-the-scenes content, or even personalised shout-outs. These incentives not only express gratitude but also encourage viewers to become part of an exclusive community.

Selecting the Right Platform

Creators have several options when it comes to crowdfunding and donation platforms. Here are two common choices:

1. Patreon: Patreon is a popular platform that allows creators to offer tiered membership levels to their supporters. Each tier comes with specific perks, and supporters can choose the level that suits them best. Patreon provides a structured way to provide ongoing value to your patrons while receiving recurring financial support.

2. Donation Links: Setting up donation links through platforms like PayPal or Ko-fi offers a more straightforward approach. Creators can place donation links in their video descriptions or on their social media profiles, allowing viewers to make one-time or recurring contributions without the need for tiered rewards.

The choice between Patreon and donation links often depends on a creator's content, audience, and preferred method of engagement.

Effective Strategies for Crowdfunding and Donations

To make the most of crowdfunding and donation opportunities, consider these strategies:

1. Transparency: Be transparent with your audience about how contributions will support your channel. Clearly communicate your goals and how their support will make a difference.

2. Exclusive Content: Offer exclusive content or perks to patrons or donors to make them feel valued and appreciated. This could include early access to videos, Q&A sessions, or personalised content.

3. Regular Updates: Keep your supporters engaged by providing regular updates on your progress, projects, and goals. Regular communication helps maintain a strong connection with your audience.

4. Promotion: Promote your crowdfunding or donation options in your videos, social media posts, and other online channels to ensure your audience is aware of these opportunities.

Ethical Considerations

Maintaining ethical standards is crucial when seeking financial support from your audience. Be transparent about how contributions will be used and ensure that any rewards or perks promised are delivered as described. Honesty and integrity build trust with your audience and encourage continued support.

Conclusion: Viewer Support as a Revenue Stream

In conclusion, crowdfunding and donations offer YouTube creators a powerful means of monetizing their channels while fostering a sense of community and connection with their audience. By selecting the right platform, offering valuable perks, and maintaining transparency, creators can harness the support of their loyal viewers in the realm of British English on YouTube. Ultimately, it's a mutually beneficial relationship where creators receive financial backing, viewers gain access to exclusive content, and both parties share in the journey of content creation.

Chapter-9

Diversify Platforms: Expand your online presence by repurposing your content on other social media platforms and driving traffic back to your YouTube channel.

Diversify Platforms: Expanding Your Online Presence Beyond YouTube

In the dynamic landscape of online content creation, diversifying your platforms is a strategic move that can amplify your reach and engagement. By repurposing your content on various social media platforms and directing traffic back to your YouTube channel, you can build a stronger online presence and cultivate a more extensive and engaged audience. In British English, let's explore the intricacies of diversifying platforms and how it can empower content creators.

The Power of Multichannel Presence

YouTube, with its massive viewership and monetization opportunities, is often the primary platform for content creators. However, relying solely on one platform can be limiting, as it confines your content to a specific audience and can make you vulnerable to changes in algorithms or policies.

Diversifying platforms involves extending your content to other social media channels like Instagram, Twitter, Facebook, TikTok, and more. This approach broadens your reach, engages with different demographics, and safeguards your content against unforeseen changes on a single platform.

Repurposing Content Strategically

Repurposing content is the art of adapting your existing videos, snippets, or related content to suit the unique characteristics and preferences of each platform. Here's how to do it effectively:

1. Tailor for Each Platform: Understand the nature of each social media platform and tailor your content accordingly. For instance, Instagram favours visual content, while Twitter emphasises concise text and hashtags.

2. Highlight Key Moments: Identify compelling or educational snippets from your YouTube videos and use them as teasers or highlights on other platforms. These snippets should pique viewers' interest and encourage them to explore the full video on your YouTube channel.

3. Leverage Platform Features: Make use of platform-specific features such as Instagram Stories, Facebook Live, or TikTok's short-form video format. These features can enhance your content's discoverability and engagement.

4. Cross-Promotion: Promote your YouTube channel and other social media profiles within your content. Encourage viewers to follow you on other platforms to stay updated.

Building a Coherent Brand

Maintaining consistency in branding, voice, and content across all platforms is crucial for audience recognition and loyalty. Your online presence should feel like a cohesive ecosystem, with each platform serving a unique purpose while aligning with your brand identity.

In British English, ensure that your tone, language, and messaging are consistent across platforms to reinforce your brand's authenticity and trustworthiness.

Engagement and Community Building

Each social media platform offers different ways to engage with your audience. Engage actively by responding to comments, participating in discussions, and fostering a sense of community. Recognize the nuances of each platform's culture and etiquette to build genuine connections with your followers.

Encourage cross-platform interactions by directing your audience from one platform to another. For example, you can host Q&A sessions on Twitter and invite viewers to submit questions from YouTube, creating a seamless flow of engagement.

Analytics and Adaptation

As you diversify platforms, track the performance of your content on each one. Analyse engagement metrics, such as likes, shares, comments, and follower growth, to identify what resonates most with your audience on each platform.

Use these insights to adapt your content strategy. If shorter, bite-sized content performs well on Instagram, consider creating more of it. If your YouTube tutorials garner significant engagement, continue to provide in-depth content for your subscribers.

Ethical Considerations

When diversifying platforms, it's essential to respect the unique policies and guidelines of each platform. Familiarise yourself with the rules related to content, promotion, and monetization to ensure ethical and compliant practices.

Conclusion: The Power of Multichannel Presence

In conclusion, diversifying your platforms by repurposing content on various social media channels is a strategic approach that can elevate your online presence as a content creator. By tailoring content, maintaining consistent branding, fostering engagement, and adapting based on analytics, you can harness the power of multichannel presence in the realm of British English on YouTube.

Diversifying platforms not only broadens your reach but also strengthens your resilience in an ever-evolving digital landscape. It empowers you to engage with diverse audiences, cultivate communities, and secure your position as a content creator across multiple platforms.

Chapter-10

Consistency and Adaptation: Maintain a consistent upload schedule while staying updated with YouTube trends and algorithm changes to ensure long-term growth and revenue.

Consistency and Adaptation: The Twin Pillars of Long-Term Success on YouTube

In the dynamic world of YouTube content creation, two crucial principles, consistency, and adaptation, stand as the cornerstones of long-term growth and revenue generation. By adhering to a consistent upload schedule and staying abreast of YouTube trends and algorithm changes, content creators can navigate the ever-evolving digital landscape and secure their position in the realm of British English on YouTube.

The Power of Consistency

Consistency in content creation is a commitment to delivering a steady stream of high-quality videos at predictable intervals. This practice benefits both creators and their audience in several ways:

1. Audience Expectations: Consistency establishes expectations among your viewers. They come to anticipate when new content will be available, making it easier for them to engage with your channel regularly.

2. Algorithm Favour: YouTube's algorithm rewards consistent uploads. Regular content release signals to the algorithm that your channel is active and invested in providing fresh content to viewers, potentially improving your visibility in search results and recommendations.

3. Viewer Loyalty: A consistent upload schedule helps build viewer loyalty. When viewers know they can rely on your channel for regular, valuable content, they are more likely to subscribe and return for future videos.

4. Improved Planning: Consistency promotes better content planning and organisation. Creators can structure their content calendar, plan ahead for special events or seasons, and maintain a steady workflow.

Adaptation to Trends and Algorithm Changes

While consistency is pivotal, it should be complemented by a proactive approach to staying updated with YouTube trends and algorithm changes. YouTube continually evolves to meet viewer preferences and market trends. To adapt effectively:

1. Monitor Trends: Regularly research and monitor trending topics, keywords, and content formats within your niche. Platforms like Google Trends and YouTube Trends can be valuable tools for this purpose.

2. Engage with Your Audience: Actively engage with your viewers through comments, surveys, or social media to understand their preferences and feedback. This insight can inform your content strategy and help you stay relevant.

3. Algorithm Awareness: Stay informed about algorithm changes and updates. YouTube often releases information about algorithm adjustments that can impact content discovery and recommendations.

4. Experimentation: Be open to experimentation. Don't be afraid to try new content formats, styles, or topics to see how they resonate with your audience. Flexibility and adaptation are key to staying relevant.

Balancing Consistency and Adaptation

Balancing consistency with adaptation can be challenging but is essential for long-term success. Here's how to strike that balance:

1. Content Planning: Create a content calendar that outlines your consistent upload schedule. Within this framework, allocate space for experimenting with new content and trends. This way, you maintain your regular content while allowing room for adaptation.

2. Regular Audits: Periodically review your content performance and audience engagement metrics. This helps you identify what's working and where you might need to adapt your strategy.

3. Feedback Loop: Foster a feedback loop with your audience. Encourage viewers to share their thoughts and suggestions, and use this feedback to refine your content approach.

4. Algorithm Updates: Stay informed about algorithm updates through official YouTube channels and industry news sources. Adjust your content strategy if necessary to align with new algorithmic preferences.

Ethical Considerations

In British English and across the YouTube community, maintaining ethical practices is paramount. Avoid resorting to clickbait, misleading thumbnails, or spammy tactics to drive views and engagement. Prioritise providing genuine value to your viewers while adapting to trends and algorithm changes.

Conclusion: The Path to Long-Term Success

In conclusion, the interplay between consistency and adaptation serves as the roadmap to long-term success and revenue generation on YouTube in the realm of British English. By maintaining a consistent upload schedule, you set clear expectations for your audience and signal your commitment to delivering valuable content.

Simultaneously, by staying updated with trends and algorithm changes, you ensure that your content remains relevant and discoverable.

Embracing these twin pillars empowers content creators to navigate the ever-evolving YouTube landscape, engage with their audience effectively, and secure a lasting presence as influential voices in their respective niches. In essence, it's a strategy that marries the reliability of consistency with the flexibility of adaptation, leading to sustained growth and revenue.

Closing summary: Your Journey To Youtube Prosperity

Closing Summary: Your Journey to YouTube Prosperity

In the vast realm of online content creation, YouTube stands as a beacon of opportunity for those with the passion and dedication to share their talents and knowledge with the world. Throughout this exploration of "10 Proven Strategies for Making Money on YouTube" in the context of British English, we've unveiled the blueprint for success in this dynamic digital landscape.

At its core, success on YouTube hinges on two pillars: authenticity and strategy. Your journey begins by selecting a content niche that resonates with your passions and expertise. This authenticity forms the foundation for attracting a dedicated audience who shares your enthusiasm.

Quality content creation is your next stride forward. Invest in the tools and skills necessary to produce videos that captivate and inform. As you refine your content, you'll draw viewers into your world, fostering a sense of connection that keeps them coming back.

Unlocking the power of SEO optimization ensures your content is discoverable in a sea of videos. Effective keywords, compelling titles, and detailed descriptions become your map to reach a broader audience.

Engaging with your viewers is your secret weapon. Building a community of dedicated followers is as valuable as any monetization strategy. Actively respond to comments, seek feedback, and create a sense of belonging among your audience.

Monetization features, such as AdSense, channel memberships, and merchandise integration, offer tangible opportunities to turn your passion into profit. Diversify your income streams to build a stable and sustainable revenue source.

Affiliate marketing and sponsorships allow you to collaborate with brands and amplify your earnings. Maintaining authenticity and transparency is paramount in building trust with your audience.

Crowdfunding and donations open the door to direct viewer support, fostering a sense of community and financial stability.

Diversifying platforms by repurposing content on other social media channels extends your reach and engagement. Consistency in content delivery and adaptation to trends and algorithm changes are the twin keys to long-term success.

As you embark on your YouTube journey in British English, remember that while financial gain is a worthy goal, it's not the sole measure of your achievement. The value you bring to your viewers, the connections you forge, and the impact you make in the digital realm are equally significant.

So, embrace these ten proven strategies with enthusiasm, dedication, and an unwavering commitment to authenticity. Your path to YouTube prosperity is a dynamic one, filled with challenges and triumphs. With these strategies as your guiding stars, may your journey be both rewarding and fulfilling as you navigate the exciting and ever-evolving world of YouTube content creation.

NOTES